ABDUL RAHMAN

Democratic Transition and Redefining Foreign Policy of Pakistan

Copyright © Abdul Rahman, 2018

All rights reserved. No part of this publication may be reproduced, stored or transmitted in any form or by any means, electronic, mechanical, photocopying, recording, scanning, or otherwise without written permission from the publisher. It is illegal to copy this book, post it to a website, or distribute it by any other means without permission.

First edition

This book was professionally typeset on Reedsy.
Find out more at reedsy.com

Contents

1

Preparation of various Political Parties

The existing circumstances are not conducive for any party as most of the mainstream parties are in disarray. There seems to be no party that may be prepared to contest the upcoming elections of 2018 with thumping majority.

Even the ruling party Pakistan Muslim League (N) has been in disarray and disintegration after the sudden disqualification of Prime Minister Nawaz Sharif in Panama Papers Case and Hudaibia papers reference. He was disqualified after the Joint Investigation Report Submitted in the Supreme Court of Pakistan.

The National Accountability Bureau was directed to file references against Ex-PM Nawaz and His Two sons Hassan & Husain Nawaz, daughter Maryam Nawaz and His Son in law Captain Retired Safdar and Current Finance Minister Ishaq Dar -The Father in the law of Nawaz's Daughter. The Nab Court was tasked to decide the Case in 6 months and announce Sentence under said Rules.

In this connection, the Nab court served notices to PM Nawaz, his Two sons, his daughter Maryam Nawaz, His Son in law Captain Safdar and Ishaque Dar the Finance Minister in the Both Cabinets of Former PM Nawaz Sharif and Current PM Shahid Khaqan Abbasi.

The First Notices did not comply and none appeared before the court to prove their Innocence. after Serving the notices Twice, NAB Court convicted the Hassan, Husain, Maryam, Captain Safdar and Nawaz Sharif.

Due to defiance of notices, Court had Issued Non-bailable warrants of Nawaz Sharif's Children and captain Safdar was arrested at the airport by the Nab authorities and later he was released on bail.

Ex-PM Nawaz Sharif appeared in the Nab court and left for the UK where his Wife Kulsoom was operated for Throat Cancer. According to his party Sources, he Will return to Pakistan in January next year. He has decided not to face the trial after conviction. Ex PM's Daughter and His Son in law are facing Trial of Panama Papers and Mayfair Flats Issue. The PML (N) also seems to be disintegrated as there have been several intra-Party differences especially the question of next party chief as Ex-PM Nawaz Sharif cannot become the party chief after disqualification by Supreme Court in Panama Papers case.

In addition, the Senate has also passed a resolution against its own of. to stop the doors for the disqualified Person to head the political party as earlier the Ruling party had been successful to get the bill passed in Senate to pave the way for Nawaz to head the party. There are also family differences between two brothers i.e Nawaz Sharif and Shahbaz Sharif as well. Nawaz wants his daughter to head the party whereas some want Shahbaz as Party chief such a situation has further confused Sharif Family.

Furthermore, The arrest of Sharjeel Memon of PPP in 6 billion corruption case by NAB, has further affected the Pakistan People's Party popularity among the people of Sindh as it has raised the eyebrows of the PPP MNAs and MPAs to change their loyalties and get themselves as the Corruption of billions of rupees unfolds.

The arrest has also sent shock waves to the PPP Co-chairman Asif Ali Zardari to discuss the matter and get efforts to get him released from the NAB.

PPP has been giving the impression that they have been targeted as NAB is aggressive Towards PPP and Flexible towards Nawaz Sharif and His family members. To some extent appeared in their opinion may have weight age as you all know that Nawaz and his family have been left for with Accountability court proceedings even Nawaz Sharif himself absconding from the Trial proceedings against him and his family.

PPP's state of affairs is further aggravated by Agha Siraj Durrani The Speaker Sindh Assembly who had insulted the Vote in a public gathering sparking a wave of protest against him through Social Media, Electronic and Print Media. People Expressed their anger strongly and condemned his remarks for the sanctity of Vote and its importance. People went to say that PPP has devalued their Vote mandate and they may face challenges in Upcoming Election of 2018 and when they reach out to the people again and seek votes for the candidates.

Even Party's Co-Chairman Asif Zardari, His Sister Faryal Talpur, and Awais Muzaffar Tappi are also facing corruption charges and soon may be booked for the cases pending against them especially the misappropriation in Development funds, awarding contracts to Bahria Town and selling Properties of millions , China cutting issues , Sale of Jobs and other cases .

These high profile figures may soon be in the grip of NAB given to their cases sensitivity.

Thirdly, The Division of MQM into two factions i.e. MQM London and MQM Pakistan has further widened the political vacuum of urban politics as earlier MQM was the major party having the urban mandate, especially from Karachi and Hyderabad. The Division was caused by Altaf Husain' Hate speech against Armed Forces and connections with Indian agency Raw which prompted action against the party's working and the Rangers commandos Raided the MQM Headquarters situated at 90 and arrested several most wanted criminals and seized a large number of sophisticated weapons bullets and other explosive material. The Rangers had also demolished MQM offices and the encroached land was evacuated with help of Rangers.

After such major offensive, MQM Pakistan was born headed by Dr Farooque Sattar. He reconstituted the Coordination Committee to escape action from Rangers.

The Division of MQM into Two factions i.e. London and Pakistan created disarray among the party and the old Party workers and candidates were divided some went in support of MQM London and Some supported the MQM Pakistan under new leadership i.e. Dr Farooque Sattar. The Division also created Space for Rebellious candidates to found a new party.

The Ex-Mayor of Karachi Mustafa Kamal intro Pakistan after self-exile and Established his own party namely Pak Sarzameen Party (PSP) and contacted the old companions of MQM to join the new party as MQM was under the influence of Altaf Hussain.

Many Notable figures joined the PSP including Anis

Kaimkhani, Raza Haroon, Dr Sagheer Ahmed, Waseem Aftab, Anees Khan advocateAfkhar Randhawa, Bilquis Mukhtar and Hundreds of MQM workers joined the New Party.

The PSP has been termed as fastest growing New Party with many well known and veteran politicians are joining the party prior to Next General Elections of 2018.

Although, the PSP has not fielded any Candidate for either seat of Provincial Seats or National Assembly Seats as it has been newly established party but experts and political pundits are of the view that in Upcoming Elections it may have more seats from urban Population of Karachi and Hyderabad and May give a tough time to MQM Pakistan. The PSP is organizing its District Base throughout the Province of Sindh in order to get support from Interior Sindh.

The PSP has also organized biggest Public gatherings in big cities such as Karachi and Hyderabad and attracted a huge number people. The party may take time to get deeply rooted in mainstream politics.

In this whole Process, the PTI seems to be well ahead of all other parties and considered the hot favourite for the upcoming General Elections of 2018, given its current pace and people friendly approach.

It is the only Party that unfolded the PPP-PML (N) Nexus of political turns through a traditional term *"Muk Muka"* to deceive the people. PTI exposed the corruption of both parties and Staged sit in and carried out long March against the alleged Rigging in the Elections of 2013 in Punjab and how PTI's mandate law of.

Jamaat Islami is also one of the moderate Islamic Parties which may influence the future Elections of 2018 as its Ameer Mr Siraj Haq has reinvigorated the party as it was in the times of Qazi Hussain Ahmed. Currently, PTI and JI have a coalition Government in KPK.

The efforts are underway by the religious parties to revive the MMA by uniting on the single platform and making the alliance of religious Parties to contest and field the joint and consensus candidates in General Elections of 2018.

In case, MMA is revived then JI may part ways from PTI but if MMA was not revived, then these two parties may remake their alliance in KP, Sindh, Punjab and Baluchistan to get maximum seats to form the Central and Provincial Governments.

As PPP has lost its vote bank in Punjab, KP, Baluchistan and PTI have been 2nd biggest Party in Punjab and leading party in KP in the last Election of 2013. Even PTI has won the NA -04 Seat recently.

PTI has been pursuing the expansion policy and they have the presence in all the four provinces including Azad Kashmir. They have got good well-known political figures and some are the Veteran PPP and PML –N stalwarts and their lookout are still on.

According to their party plan, they want to contest every seat in every province of Pakistan -be it Provincial Assembly or National Assembly or Senate.

The Smaller parties such as JUI, ANP, PML Q and PML (F) etc are not in position to clean sweep the election but they may get their seats wherever these have influenced such as JUI in KPK and convicted the ANP in KPK and Karachi, PML (Q) in Punjab and the PML (F) in Sindh .

These Parties will join the coalition of such party that will get the clear majority to form the Government as in Past it is evident from their alliances Especially, MQM, JUI and PML (F) intend to be the part of Govt either at provincial Level or in

Central Government.

Although, JUI is a Religious party, yet it has remained coalition partner with PPP and currently in PML (N) led Govt. Similarly, MQM has remained the coalition partner with PPP.

Hence, after a detailed analysis, we have found that PML(N) has been baffled by NAB references, PPP has not organized itself in Punjab, Parties are KP, Baluchistan. PPP may take seats in Sindh especially the areas where it has more influence at home constituencies where PPP backed candidates have been winning for many years such as Larkana, Sukkur, Shikarpur, Jacobabad, Dadu, Nawabshah etc.

In this context, PTI is well prepared to sweep the upcoming General Elections as the ground is empty and PTI has to work out on a rigorous Plan to get the majority to form the government.

PTI has upper hand in existing circumstances unless there is any possible deal between the PPP and PML (N) as these two parties are well known to have such secret deals to put dust in the eyes of People as we have seen the friendly opposition in the current government.

PTI should have strong candidates especially in Sindh to provide oppressed people of Sindh with an option to get rid of corrupt PPP that has played with their fortune and swallowed their development budget and even insulted the Votes given by the people of Sindh on basis of votes, they were put in power but in return they have given the dusty and bumpy roads, sewage-filled cities and flooded streets. There is no name of Merit and Jobs are sold like hot cakes in millions of rupees.

In Sindh, to Succeed PTI has to approach the Feudal, land-lords Tribal chieftains and Sayeds who make up of 90 per cent of MPAs in Sindh along with Minorities. Only, non-corrupt people may be included in the party.

Finally, it all depends upon the Election Commission of Pakistan to hold a free, fair and transparent election by Implementing Electronic Voting machines and Biometric Machines to League the chances of rigging and bogus voting.

The Army may be deployed in and outside the polling stations so that law and order situation may be improved. The Polling stations may be linked through GIS system so that polling locations may track through GPS.

The Upcoming Government will have to address the issue of Load shedding if left unresolved by current regime , Economy, IMF loan Repayments, Terrorism Issue, Governance, Education and Health Sector Improvement and More Importantly to devise an effective foreign Policy of Pakistan on basis equality where the nation may not be forced to do more despite doing enough and having rendered unlimited sacrifices in fighting Terrorism .

2

The Uncertainty Surrounding General Elections 2018

Pakistan has been going through very tough times especially the disintegrated Political parties raising questions regarding the Upcoming General Elections since the main Political parties specially PML-N Leadership has been in disarray ever since the Elected Prime Minister Mian Nawaz Shareef was disqualified on the charges of corruption and Mayfair flats ownership issue as well as Panama Papers Issue. The national accountability Bureau has woke up after a long period of dormancy and started actions against high profile Cases specially Shareef Family and related leaders.

All the parties enjoy watching Shareef Family being dragged to the accountability courts for prosecution. The Supreme court orders for Probe against Mian Nawaz Sharif ,His Two sons Hassan and Husain Nawaz , His Daughter Mariam Nawaz , His Close Relative Ishaq Dar and His Son in law Captain Safdar for their alleged involvement in illegal Money transfer , tax Evasion and Illegal Property purchased through transferring the Black money by establishing Offshore companies in UK .

The charges against Shareef Family Members are very serious as Nawaz's sons and Ishaq Dar are absconding from the NAB proceedings whereas Mian Nawaz Shareef along with her Daughter and son in law Captain Safdar are facing Corruption charges in the NAB courts and as per the orders of the Supreme court of Pakistan, NAB has been given the 6 Months time to decide the cases against the Shareef Family and take the Panama case to its logical End by punishing the Perpetrators of The Crime.

Meanwhile, PTI has also lost their main wicket when MNA Mr Jahangir Tareen was disqualified over Tax evasion and submission of Fake Asset Details and Paying less Tax on his Agriculture Production and having the Offshore company that was not declared as his assets at the time filing his nomination.

Luckily, The Captain of PTI was absolved from the charges of having received foreign Funds in the name of charity or welfare activities with special reference to Shaukat Khanum Cancer Hospital.

Given the disqualification of Jahangir Tareen, PTI has suffered great loss as its main financer who funded the most of the party activities was disqualified by the Apex Court through a Petition filed by PMl-N Leader Hanif Abbasi.

PTI is being considered the favourite for upcoming General Elections of 2018 as it has emerged as the 3rd largest Political party after PML-N and PPP. But with the disqualification of Its General Secretary MNA Jahangir Tareen, It might have suffered a setback but luckily the Chairman PTI was absolved of the charges.

JUI and Jamaat Islami are also main religious Political Parties having roots in Politics across Pakistan especially, JUI in KPK and Baluchistan whereas Jamaat Islami in Punjab and KPK as Jamaat Islami, currently, is in alliance with PTI in Provincial Govt of KPK.

The Religious parties are trying to revive the –the MMA (Muttahida Majlis Amal) but in current political arena, it would be very difficult to form a religious Alliance as Most of the religious Parties have loyalties with mainstream Political parties such as Jamaat Islami with PTI and JUI Fazal with PML –N and In past –With PPP led Government . If the Religious parties succeed in the revival of MMA then this will be the great setback for all the partied i.e PTI, PPP and PML-N.

While other Political parties such as MQM, PSP, PML – Q, PML-F and ANP are not strong enough to make the Provincial or Central Government but they will rather prefer to be part of a coalition with the party having a clear majority to form the Government at the Centre and The Provincial Level. At the Moment , as per the Survey conducted by Gallop and Pildat , the Parties which are considered favorite for Upcoming General Elections 2018 are PTI in KPK , Punjab , Sindh , Jamaat Islami in KPK , Punjab and Baluchistan , MQM,PSP ,PML-F in Sindh specially the urban areas of Karachi , Hyderabad , Mirpurkhas , Sukkur as these parties are also the part of GDA –Grand Democratic Alliance . It is also said that in the upcoming General Elections 2018, Independent Candidates will also play their role as their number will be very high in future.

The Elections Reforms Bill was the only hurdle in holding the Elections on time that was luckily passed from NA and Senate. The Election Commission will soon start the exercise of Delimitation of the Constituencies on the basis of Census 2017 Statistics. The Election Reforms Bill 2017 was much-echoed Issue in the National Assembly and Senate as PPP was aggressive against the Census Results as they were raising objections against the Census Results and wanted the Elections on old Constituencies and opposed the delimitation exercise. But the consensus rejected the rumours of Delay in Polls or Early Polls. The Political Pundits and Experts are of the View, given the Passage of Election Reforms Bill from both Houses, the Signs of holding elections are becoming clear.

But the Preparation of the parties is still a far cry as No party is ready or organized to contest General Elections 2018 due to Political Crisis and Prevalent Accountability Proceedings against the Leaders of Various Parties specially PML-N, PPP and PTI. However, The Political parties i.e PTI, Jamaat Islami, PSP or GDA in Sindh may sweep Seats from Rural and Urban areas of Sindh and form Provincial Government as well. But so far it seems to be very difficult parties to defeat PPP in Sindh as it enjoys Monopoly in Sindh as it has not faced any strong Opposition in the last several Years. GDA may work if PTI becomes the part of it.

Despite all this, The uncertainty still prevails regarding General polls and There are some reports of Technocrat Government to be installed but Political parties especially PTI, Jamaat Islami or Even PPP will strongly resist if such move or plan was unearthed or Establishment played any role in the forming Government in General Elections.

As precedence was available with MQM-PSP romance to contest Election on the same platform with joint Election Symbol but the romance didn't last long with PSP leader Mustafa Kamal spilt beans regarding Establishment role for Merger or coalition to keep PPP, PML-N out of Mainstream Politics. It is also expected that there may be coalition Government as No party will have any clear majority to form their Government in the centre or at Province, given their weak political Organization and Activities especially, several forward Blocks are likely to be formed in PML-N and PPP. As per vote bank, PTI has climbed the 2nd Position as per recent by-election results.

Whatever, result or outcome of Panama papers or NAB References against Shareef Family should be, But it is clear that PML–N may not form a government in Upcoming Elections Except they may clinch some seats in Punjab, given the Development Projects Initiated by Punjab Chief Minister Shahbaz Sharif.

Unfortunately, the sword of Disqualification looms upon him due to Model Town Massacre Case and the decision may go against him as Awami Tehreek Leader, Tahir ul-Qadri has announced to hold Protests and Sit-ins Dharnas until the resignation of Punjab CM and Law Minister Rana Sanuallah. Let's wait and see what happens next but people opine with the uncertainty that the Election on time, will be a distant dream owing to prevailing Political Scenario and preparation.

3

Senate Chairman Election 2018

Elections always witnessed a question mark due to horse trading, rigging, bartering and bidding. The recent Senate Elections 2018 were no Exception as The Senate Elections were held in sheer contradiction where many Mainstream Political parties such as PTI, MQM cried Foul play and horse trading in the Elections especially the PPP's grabbing of Two Senate Seats from KPK on the basis of 6 MPAs was beyond Understanding and opened the Pandora box as how a Party having only 6 MPAs could manage to win two seats from KPK .On the Other hand, MQM-P due to infighting lost the seats and managed to grab a single seat from Sindh while PML-N swept all the seats from Punjab and Islamabad.

If we go through the current Senate party-wise position, PML-N Leads the House with 34 Senate Seats as one independent candidate announced to join PML-N, followed by PPP and PTI having 20 and 12 Seats each. However, Ten Independent candidates from FATA may play the deciding role for The election of Senate Chairman as PML-N needs 19 More Seats to get his Nominee elected out of 104 seat Upper House.

The PPP and PTI contacts are also reported as both partied

contacted the CM Baluchistan for Alliance. The PTI demands Deputy chairman whereas chairman slot is offered to PPP Nominee. But the recent party meet up withdraws the decision as they were of the view that having alliance with either PPP or PML-N would pour water on their long struggle against Corruption and corrupt politicians as Chairman PTI believed that having alliance with PPP may benefit PML-N and other opposition parties including JUI-F who are the strong critics of both parties . They may launch a public campaign against the party's vision that those who used to call Zardari (Bemari) The Disease for Sindh now sitting in their ranks and made an alliance with the corrupt party in quest of Power. Suppose, If they make an alliance, they will have 32 seats, they will still require 21 seats to get the Slot of Senate Chairman. Zardari is eying 15 Independent candidates of FATA and Baluchistan, National Party of Baluchistan's 5 seats, MQM's 5 Seats, PML-F 1 seat, JI 2 Seats etc. If Zardari succeeds in getting the small parties on board then it will give tough time to PML-N. JUI-F has announced to back PMl-N Nominee whereas JI may support PTI as both parties are running a coalition Govt in KP.

PPP has enjoyed the coalition with MQM-P past through this political bonhomie did not last longer owing to the greed of power and resources on the part of MQM and contradictory Separate Province Demands and tirade against Pakistan by self-exiled MQM –London chief Altaf Hussain.

As regards The Senate Elections, they are also reported to be rigged since Billions of Rupees were used to influence and change the loyalties of MNAs and MPAs. Though the ECP has taken the Notice of such gross irregularities, yet No action may likely be taken owing expiry of the Government Term in May 2018.

PML-N may win Chairman Senate Seat Either from its allies or PML-N owing to the consensus on Nominee, while PPP claims to have 60 Seats including FATA senators. But PML-N has not reached the decision of Final Candidate. In this situation, all the parties appear to be divided struggling to find the suitable candidate after refusal and Rejection over the name of Existing Senate Chairman, Senator Raza Rabbani by Zardari Though the recommendation card was played by PML-N former chief Mian Nawaz Shareef. Shareefs are in disarray after disqualification as PM and Party chief altogether.

They have already started anti-Judiciary, NAB and Armed forces agitation campaign are not in the good books of Establishment as well. However, as they enjoy the majority in the upper House, they face less resistance or effort to get their nominee elected.

So far, the PML-N leadership has not been able to finalize their Nominee for Senate Chairman and Deputy Chairman Slots as they are still doing the consultation with key allies such as National Party of Baluchistan NP, JUI-F and Others.

PTI and PPP, on the other hand, are also seen busy to form an alliance to get the Slots. PPP's Co-chairman Former President, Asif Ali Zardari is alleged to have bought the MPAs and MNAs and this purchase process is said to be continued as Senators are being offered millions as per News reports to Support their nominee for Chairman slot.

PPP appears to be the only party that is in close contact with the independent candidates and had negotiations with various Main Stream and Small parties Sindh, KP, Baluchistan to reach on an agreement for winning support from the allies for their PPP nominee likely Salim Mandiwala etc.

On the other hand, PTI is vying for Deputy chairman slot

as they enjoy the third position in Upper House. Both PTI-PPP may reach on consensus candidate Sadiq Sanjrani as both parties have consensus over Sadiq Sanjrani He is emerging as the favourite candidate for the opposition in Upper House. Therefore, PTI finally nods to support PPP candidate after having internal party discussions and Demand the Deputy Chairman Slot.

The Ball is in the PML-N's court as they have the majority and only require 18 seats to win the chairman Slot. With JUI –F support and eying independent senators they may still be able to win The Chairman Senate seat but this prediction may be bit early as anything happens at any time. Maybe, The PPP succeeds in making allies and winning support as Zardari is very clever in making surprises or stunning the opposition.

Zardari is also considered the king of changing the game as he did in Baluchistan by toppling the Zahri Govt and bringing in New set up in Baluchistan.PTI will support PPP Nominee as both parties are against the PML-N Government. The Political Pundits say that if Zardari's Candidate wins that will be the great set back or Blow for PML-N.

The Election for the appointment of Chairman and Deputy Chairman Senate is scheduled Tomorrow, so let's wins the Elections of Upper House Head and Deputy Head -be it PML-N or PPP-PTI allies. But Zardari has shown disappointment over the proposed name of Sadiq Sanjrani for Chairman Slot during the Meeting of CM Baluchistan Abdul Qayoom Bizenjo and PTI Chief Imran Khan.

4

Senate Chairman Election 2018

Elections in Pakistan have always been marred by turmoil, rigging, horse trading, nepotism, favouritism, manipulation and bartering of votes.

The Voters are influenced and threatened to face dire consequences if they did not vote and support any specific Party Leader usually a traditional Feudal who even warns to forcibly displace or disappear any person if they or their favourite candidate was not voted. In the past several decades, Pakistan has never witnessed any free, fair and transparent elections.

However, The Elections held in 1988 under Army are said to be the fair ones as people believe that people were given free choice to vote for their Favourite candidates. Luckily, PPP under Benazir with simple majority formed their Government.

Afterwards, PPP and PML-N had their turns one after another and maintained their duopoly until General Parvez Musharraf's Toppling of PML-N second Government when his Plane was denied landing and Even The Army chief was changed in his absence while he was on the official visit.

The Army supported their General and helped him become the Marshal Law administrator and then President after Holding a Public Referendum.

Musharraf enjoyed the largest tenure as Martial Law Administrator and then President of Pakistan After General Zial Haque who had enjoyed the largest tenure as both Martial Law Administrator and Then President. Though, later he declared that he had not imposed any Martial law.

It is Irony that Pakistan has experienced mostly Military Coups than Civilian Governments as a result we had Iskandar Mirza, General Ayoob Khan, General Yahya, General Zial Haq, Zulfiquar Ali Bhutto and Musharraf as CMLAs though General Musharraf Declared that It was not Martial Law but when he imposed Emergency in the country and kept the constitution in abeyance . The people called it Martial Law or Military Rule as the constitution was suspended.

His reforms especially for improving and reforming Local Governance System and an introduction of New Local Governance system in which Commissionerate System was replaced with District Governments where the District Nazim was the Most Powerful Administrator whereas a Grade 20 Officer worked as District coordination officer to ensure coordination between the Various Departments.

Each Department was headed by a grade 19/20 Officer as Executive District officer such as EDO (finance and Planning) EDO (education) EDO (Health), EDO (Revenue) EDO (Agriculture) and So. It was the first time that Finance Department was devolved at District Level which benefitted the People since each Departmental Budget was released from Account-IV of District instead of Account-I i.e. Provincial Government.

The District Nazim with help of EDO(F&P) prepared their

own budget and approved the required schemes upon the recommendation of the District Council members and thus over 80 % of the allocated budget was utilized. Such Utilization changed the shape of Urban and Rural areas and Development was evident from the Massive Development schemes and their Proper Implementation.

The Mayor Karachi, Naimutullah Khan did the best and changed the whole scenario of Karachi and made a very Clean and Green City and later the MQMs Mustafa Kamal became Mayor Karachi and targeted the own areas for Development.

Musharraf held a so-called referendum and got himself elected as President and then Held Elections in which his party PML Q came into power and formed the Government in Sindh, Center and Punjab. Then in his era, Benazir Bhutto was assassinated and he was held responsible for Benazir Killing. The Country experienced bloody Riots as the angry mobs set the Govt Buildings, Banks, Schools and Police Station on fire and there was Chaos all-around since Musharraf had stopped the Security Personnel not to resist or stop the Protesters who were protesting against the Brutal Killing of their Leader Benazir Bhutto.

At least Benazir Bhutto was successful to make Musharraf as a civilian President when he was compelled through Political Pressure to withdraw from Military Uniform.

PPP won 2008 Election owing to sympathy vote and Yousuf Raza Gillani Became the Prime Minister and then Musharraf was given Clear passage to leave the country and Zardari became the President of Pakistan and completed their Tenure of Five Years. Even Supreme court disqualified Gillani over defiance to Write a letter to Swiss Government to Freeze the

Bank accounts of Zardari by awarding 30-second Sentence. Thus, Raja Parvez Ashraf replaced him as PM.

It was the first time that any Democratic Government had completed its tenure, As earlier, none was able to complete their tenure since most of the civilian governments lasted for 2 to three years hardly which were either dissolved by the presidents under articles 58 2B or ousted by CMLAs.

Then in 2013, PML –N came to power and Formed their Government and Mian Mohammad Nawaz Sharif Became the only Person in the History who had become the PM third time in Pakistan. As PPP Government had brought 18th Amendment and made the way for the PM third time to hold the Office and given Provincial Autonomy.

The PML N- Government came under fire when PTI complained that there was rigging in General Elections. Even the Speaker NA Ayaz Sadique was disqualified and there was re-poll on his constituency but he re-won the seat and became the Speaker again. The Model town incident and Long March and Dharnas became the order of the Day and then the tremors of Panama Leaks shook the world hard and The Names of Mian Nawaz Sharif, His Sons Hassan and Hussain Nawaz and Her daughter came in corruption list of Panama Papers. All the Parties Started protests and demanded resignation from Nawaz Sharif but his stubbornness cost him a lot and he was disgraced publically when he was disqualified on 20th April 2017 by Supreme Court of Pakistan after the JIT findings in Panama Papers Case.

Nawaz's Bad luck did not stop here, He was sentenced on Friday, July 6, 2018, for Ten Years and His Daughter Mariam Nawaz for 7 Years and His Son law Captain Safdar for one Year in Aven Field Reference Filed by NAB under Directions of Supreme court of Pakistan.

With Elections 2018 are just three days Away, All the Political Parties are busy in their Election campaigns. Some of The Election rallies are targeted by Suicide Bombings in Mastung and Among the dead were the Workers of Baluchistan Awami Party) including the party's provincial candidate, Siraj Raisani whereas in Peshawar Suicide Attack ANP Leader for Provincial Seat Haroon Ahmed Bilour was killed and other Party workers were also Killed in the Suicide Blast.

The Political Pundits and Analysts are of the View that the PTI enjoys a Strong position in KPK, Punjab and Sindh followed by Alliance of Religious Parties (Muttahida Majlis e-Amal) MMA has also the strong position in KPK, Punjab, Sindh and Baluchistan. The Baluchistan is Center for religious parties and has always Mix support for Nationalists such as Baluchistan Awami Party, National Party of Pakistan, JUI, PPP and PML – N.

In Sindh, the Old Parties such as MQM has the stronghold in Urban Population of Karachi, Hyderabad, Mirpur Khas whereas PPP has Strength in Interior Sindh. They are facing strong Resistance from Grand Democratic Alliance headed by PML-Functional Head Pir Pagara and other Nationals. Though MQM has seat adjustment with GDA, yet MQM has always preferred to be in power be it PPP or PML-Q. The Other new Force is Pak Sarzameen Party (PSP) Headed by Mustafa Kamala. The Party consists the old stalwarts of MQM who left MQM after differences with Farooque Sattar and joined PSP. This would be the First Election for them to contest and prove their Strength.

It is estimated that GDA will grab more than 40 Seats in Sindh and form their Government in Sindh and will be recognized as an Alternate Force to PPP. It is very difficult to break the Monopoly of PPP in Sindh yet People are hopeful that they will get rid of PPP hegemony forever and will prefer Service Delivery. If PTI forms an alliance with GDA in Sindh, With National Party in Baluchistan and with MMA in Punjab, KPK and Baluchistan, it will easily form Government and both PPP and PML-N will sit in opposition benches.

Despite all this, it will be very difficult to make any prediction before General Election 2018 but as per the Social Media Surveys, Gallup Pakistan Surveys and Media Debates, It is assumed that PTI will have the lion's share in NA and PA Seats in KPK, Punjab, Sindh and Baluchistan followed by MMA and GDA in Sindh. The sympathy vote may play a role for PML-N as their Leader Mian Nawaz Shareef is in Adiala jail along with his daughter as there is no any other chance for them as they were tested thrice by the People of Pakistan. PTI has brighter and stronger position to sweep the GE-2018 and Elect Imran Khan as Next PM of Pakistan Let July 25, 2018, come and decide the Future of mainstream parties i.e PTI, PPP, PML-N or MMA who will be the Next PM. Let's Wait for Elections Results to pour in.

5

Democratic Transition And Prospects For PTI in 2018

Pakistan is Going to win today as Our Voters proved by giving tough time to their Leaders who went to them for canvassing. People quizzed the candidates that first give Account of their Previous Tenure of Five years and then ask for Votes.

The New Set of Lies came while influencing the People and getting Support from the Voters But this time the voters were not deceived as they were well prepared, given the Media Reports, Political Debates and Social Media Findings as well as the Surveys that drove the last nail in the coffin and established the winning trends of the various Parties specially PTI ,PPP and PML –N

The Candidates appeared helpless before the People during the Political campaigning. There were New faces who entered in the Politics very first time and Those who made alliances on the basis to defeat PPP in Sindh to provide an alternative for the

Prosperity of Sindh especially in Education and Health Sectors. The Infrastructure also needs to be improved and as well as overall Governance Model. There is great Need of altering Centralized Local Governance System as Local Governance is considered as basic Democracy and the choice of people.

With PSP and GDA making their Debut as Alternative Forces followed by Religious Parties Alliance (Muttahida Majlis-Amal)MMA appear as Strong Contestants and may grab sufficient Seats all over Pakistan Especially in KPK, Baluchistan, Punjab and Sindh.

In this entire contest, PTI leads the rest based on the Social Surveys, Gallup Pakistan Surveys, Surveys conducted by Various Media Houses such as Dawn, Geo TV and Duniya TV.

The Main contest is between PTI, PPP, PML-N and the Independent candidates. The political parties have left the vacuum in Baluchistan as No mainstream party staged any Political Rally and There was no any Mass Political Gathering from any leading Political Party I.e PTI, PPP or PML –N Except Baluchistan Awami Party, National Party of PkMAP and MMA.

The Causes may be the Ongoing incidents of Suicide Attacks as Happened in Mastung where death Toll surpassed 100 Including the Great Leader Siraj Raisani of BAP. Peshawar Suicide Attack gobbled Haroon Bilour and other Party ANP. The latest was of Sardar Ikramullah Gandapur of PTI killed in a Suicide Attack in DI Khan along with other Party Workers. This insecure environment forced many parties to limit their Political activities as they could not risk the precious lives of their Party Leaders as well as their energetic workers.

Despite all odds, All the parties tried to reach the Voters and Presented their Political Manifestos before the People. The Manifestos were full of the new and the old Promises such as the creation of Jobs, Improving Education and Health Sectors. Improving Infrastructure and Communication gateways. There were also reports of busying and selling of Votes through Money in Some parts of the Country.

With ECP tasked with a mammoth National Duty assisted by Great Polling Staff (Trained and Groomed) as well as given the First Class Magistrate Powers and Secured by Police and Pak Army Personnel at the Polling Station , It is estimated that there would be peaceful environment all around at all the Polling stations especially those Polling Stations that are declared as "Most Sensitive" where CCTV cameras have been Installed for monitoring the Polling process and avert any untoward situation throughout the country.

Even Army has also been given the Magistrate Powers to make security arrangements at all the Polling Stations. The Best thing the ECP has done that is "RMS" Results Management System powered by NADRA Experts.

The Presiding Officers were also trained during their Two days Training regarding "RTS" Result Transmission System. The Dedicated and hardworking Team of Master Trainers and NADRA Personnel were engaged to train the polling Staff regarding the use of Android-Based ECP RTS Application and the way to transmit NA and PA results to ours, PEC of the Respective Provinces and the ECP Headquarters Islamabad.

These applications were activated by ROs one day prior to the Poll Day. RTS will prove transparent and timely Result Transmission and it will contribute to the immediate Result consolidation Polling Station wise by Taking Screenshot of Form-45 Result of account.

Truly, the Credit goes to ECP for imparting training to the Polling Staff through the Development Partners UNDP and

DAI throughout Pakistan. The Dedicated and Experienced Masters Trainers were hired to fulfil that Mammoth Task and The task was achieved quite nicely above 100% in Sindh, Punjab, KPK and Baluchistan, The Polling Staff is ready to undertake today's polling Proceedings in a Professional Manner and with pride.

The field force of Polling Staff will be assisted by the Police, The Rangers and the Army to ensure law and order within 400 Square Meter Radius. The Voting time will start from 8:00 Am and will continue without break till 6:00 PM. The Results are expected to Start Pouring In by 7:00 PM or 8:00 PM and fill the Television Screens.

As per the updated list of The Election Commission of Pakistan, There are total 3,459 candidates contesting for 272 general seats of the National Assembly whereas 8,396 are running for 577 general seats of the four provincial assemblies of Pakistan.

The National Assembly has total 342 Seats including 60 seats reserved for Women and 10 for Minorities. The Number of directly elected members is 272. The Majority Party is required to obtain at least 172 Seats to have simple Majority to form Government at Centre. The Number of reserved seats for women and Minorities may be inclusive in 172 Seats.

Punjab enjoys the huge number of NA seats i.e 183, followed by Sindh 75, KPK 43 plus 12 Fata seats after Merger the Total becomes 55, Baluchistan 17 and Federal Capital 2. That means the parties will consolidate on Punjab, the high number of NA seats, Sindh and KPK as the third in a row.

If PTI wins 130 General Seats, 30 Women and Minority Seats and 20 Independents join them, they will definitely form their independent Government without any coalition partners.

It falls short, then the alliances with MMA, GDA, Baloch National Parties, MQM or PSP could not be ruled out as PPP appears far behind on national front since they have fielded insufficient candidates in Punjab despite having 183 Seats more than required Simple Majority i.e 172 Seats.

With Leadership in Prison and Disarray, PML-N has not run their Election Campaign Effectively except media campaigns. The Media Campaigns were huge by PPP and PML-N, Moderate by PTI and MMA.

Moreover, for provincial assemblies, there are 4,036 candidates contesting for 297 general seats of the Punjab Assembly; 2,252 candidates will contest 130 general seats of the Sindh Assembly; 1,165 will compete for 99 KP Assembly seats and 943 will contest for 51 general seats of the Baluchistan Assembly.

If PTI grabs maximum seats from Punjab, KPK and few seats from Sindh, it will definitely form Government in KPK, Punjab and with GDA in Sindh. But it is up to the Voters who they vote for and who they want as Next PM of Pakistan.

Since their votes will decide the Fate of Imran Khan, Bilawal Bhutto or Shahbaz Sharif as their PM for Next Five Years. These Elections are very vital to resolve the issues such as weakening of Rupee against the dollar Since it will be the tough challenge for the Finance Minister of the New Government, Followed By Energy crisis, law and Order, Education, Health and Construction of New Dams for Electricity Generation and overcoming the Power Shortfall.

Whoever becomes the Next PM, he will have to solve the long-standing issues and bring Prosperity in Pakistan. He will have to revisit the foreign Policy, Internal Policy, water Policy and Economic Policy to carve them to suit the needs of the country and ensure Service Delivery.

6

Challenges Before New Premeir

With PTI Emerging as single Majority Party has more than 115 NA seats and More than 124 PA seats in Punjab, 65 PA seats in KP and Second Major Party in Sindh with 22 PA Seats, PTI Chairman is well prepared to be the Prime Minister of Pakistan. The Idea of "Naya Pakistan" worked and people left their comfort zone and voted for change.

After, overall seat analysis, PTI is well in position to form Government in Center, Punjab and KP.While PML-N 62 NA Seats, 130 PA seats of Punjab and PPP as third with 39 NA seats and 68 PA seats of Sindh and will like form government in Sindh.

Furthermore, PTI will sit on Opposition benches in Sindh possibly giving tough time to PPPP to improve their performance Since MQM was bit humble or friendly with PPP as the City Mayor Belonged to their Party in the previous tenure.

In today's Public address, PTI Chief (Future PM) said that he was the only leader ever to be targeted personally but buried all rifts, the differences and has completely wiped out his Past differences with people. He further clarified that he will not pursue the Policy of Victimization either.

He projected his clear vision that he will establish close brotherly relations with All the major Islamic Countries Especially Saudi Arabia, Iran, Turkey and will play his role to diffuse tensions between Saudi Arab and Iran. He stressed that the rule of law to be the top priority before his Government.

He was reported as saying that PTI government will focus on Education, Health, Police Reforms, Job creation, Fiscal Policy, Foreign Policy and Best Governance Model that suits the Democratic Trend and the Model of Pakistan. He specially hinted to involve 200 Pakistanis working abroad to reform the institutions to be made functional on modern Lines.

The first Challenge to PTI is the implementation of Uniform Education Policy in all the four provinces. It is suggested that Education is made Federal Subject having uniformity in Curriculum and its foundation in international Standards. Secondly, the promotion of Scientific Research and Technology in all the Four provinces including GB.

The Establishment of New Universities throughout Pakistan in the Lines of NAMAL college Mianwali. The Scholarships may be offered to the Deserving students so that they may face the problem of lack Funds for Studies. Establishing and creating Job Markets so that the university graduates may not face problem in getting jobs. Offering Scholarships for M.Phil and PhD Members of public Universities as well as for the talented Students to further their research in their respective fields.

The Establishment of New Hospitals in each Taluka Head Quarter and District Head Quarters and up gradation of existing Hospitals and equipping them with Modern facilities. Establishment of Cancer Hospital in every province to facilitate the Cancer patients and ensure their treatment free of Cost.

Introducing Health cards or Insurance for the patients with Fatal diseases. The Health insurance will cover their treatment costs.

The Energy crisis has been very critical in Pakistan due to Demand and Supply GAP. PTI has to spearhead the Construction of New Dams such as Bhasha and Mohammad Dams since these have been cleared by Chief Justice of Pakistan, Justice Saquib Nisar that need to be constructed on Public-Private Node.

He even established the Dams Construction Fund. PTI can further the fundraising so that construction work must be started on time. The load-shedding problem is very old even PML-N has not resolved the Load shedding issue. As the PML-N leadership, Nawaz Shareef and Shahbaz Shareef told white lies with the Simple people Pakistan that the issue of Load shedding will be resolved by 2018 but people of Pakistan are still experiencing Load unresolved. PTI has to solve the core issue on war footing basis so that prosperity could be brought in Pakistan and the Textile & Garments Industry of Karachi and Faisalabad could be revitalized.

The third biggest challenge is the depreciation of Rupee against Dollar. The Economist team should be engaged with the composition of Senior and young economists and to do the spade work for viable and sustainable Economic policy. In this connection, the services of Policy Think Tanks specially Sustainable Development Policy Institute (SDPI) Islamabad would be the key to give the best policy advise and great Professional Asad Umar would be Instrumental in this regard as well.

The Fourth Biggest challenge is the devising of Internal policy and Foreign Policy for Pakistan. it is imperative that Pakistan should adopt a clear foreign Policy and determine new terms of Engagement with US, Russia and our old friend neighbour China. Execution and acceleration of CPEC Projects must improve the Infrastructure of Pakistan.

The Fifth biggest challenge is to gain access to International Markets to improve and increase exports of Pakistan such as Grains, Fruits, Textiles and Garments. Establishing Industrial Zones and Economic zones and functioning of Gawadar Port. The Improvement of Communication, Highways, Railways and Airways especially restructuring of PIA and Pakistan Steel.

The Sixth largest challenge is the Governance Model especially the Local Governance. This should be a federal subject so that there should be a uniform local governance Model. The Experts should be engaged to study the standard local Governance Models and adopt or devise the models given needs and requirements local People.

There is also the issue of security at Loc with India owing to The Kashmir Dispute. Even the so-called Indian Media dubbed the Victory of Imran Khan as a bad omen for India due to their bonhomie with PML-N. PML-N has always maintained friendly relations with the compromise on the Kashmir. In this connection, PTI initiatives to highlight the issue in the light of UN for its resolution.

If all these issues are resolved, the people of Pakistan will have the positive image about PTI and its visionary leadership. People have trusted PTI leadership and Hopefully, PTI won't breach the trust.

People Voted for the Change and they just want to reap the fruits of change and see Pakistan as the country where the unemployment, security issues, Education issues, Health issues, bad Governance should be wiped as per their Slogan of *Naya Pakistan*.

There should be zero tolerance for corruption and The Institutions such as NAB, ACE and FIA may take action against any person if he is found involved with clear evidence.

There should also be strict laws for Corruption and befitting punishment will be meted out as was done with former PM Nawaz and his Daughter Mariam Safdar and Captain Safdar.

It is clear from their sentence that no matter how powerful the corrupt people are, they would be executed in a similar fashion.

There should be a congenial environment for the Foreign Direct Investment FDI and the boosting of the Hotel and Tourism Industry as done by UAE and Malaysia etc. Hope IK will his promises and Challenges of Pakistan with a dedicated and professional team.

7

Redefining Foreign Policy of Pakistan

Pakistan's Foreign Policy has always remained the Arab Centric with Saudi Arab having a Central role and Even its alignment towards the US since Independence. Pakistan has never revisited its Foreign Policy holistically to suit the Needs of the country on an independent approach.

Since Independence, Pakistan has never clarified its stance on Foreign Policy development and the Terms of Engagement with its neighbours and the big powers. That was why Pakistan's First Prime Minister Liaquat Ali Khan Preferred the US than Russia for its Friendship and paid his visit to America and became the part of West Block than East Block ie the then USSR.

Though Pakistan played a pivotal role in Russia-Afghan war partnership did not bear any fruit for the nation due to Political instability, Strong Military Intervention and weak fiscal Policies.

This Diplomatic relationship or bonhomie has never proved Fruitful for the country owing to America being a fair weather Friend as Pak-US relations have always been marred by Distrust.Even Security Aid offered to Pakistan by America affected its Independent Foreign Policy to the used aid as a pressure tool to force Pakistan to do More to combat terrorism and remove Safe haven of terrorists within Pakistan Domain. Although, Pakistan laid down numerous sacrifices of Soldiers and Civilians; approximately over 100000 in so-called War against Terrorism. Pakistan has already paid a heavy price to be an Ally of Pakistan.

Especially, American led NATO strikes on Afghanistan in which Pakistan was asked to cooperate and hand over the Airports and Roads for Transportation of weapons to Afghanistan for NATO forces to topple Taliban Government and to kill or capture Osama Bin Ladin -The Master Mind of 9/11 Strike on World Trade Centre. American president Bush attacked Afghanistan to avenge the 9/11 incident and to please his fellow Americans. Ever since the Strike, Afghanistan is still unstable despite the passage of 17 years of American led NATO Forces Presence. Even Taliban control 40 % of Afghanistan till today. There is no peace and frequents Suicide attacks on NATO forces and civilians have become the order of the day.

America is losing the Afghan war against terrorism badly but it resorts to blaming Pakistan for Terrorist Safe Haves along the Durand line and its fiasco in Afghan War is being associated with Pakistan but the statistics suggest that Pakistan has suffered a lot than the US. Hundreds of Civilians and Soldiers were killed in Suicide Bomb blasts on Mosques, Churches, Temples, Schools and other Political Rallies.

This happened because Pakistan cooperated with the US in Afghanistan allowing it to use Pakistan's soil against the Taliban. Such cooperation enraged Taliban against Pakistan and they become fierce enemies of Pakistan - especially its brave Armed forces who initiated their major offensive against these

Extremists in shape of Operation Zarb-e-Azb and Operation
Rad-ul-Fassad which broke their Waist and Pakistan returned
to peace. The Pak-Aghan border became the route for Aghan
Taliban to penetrate in KPK and Punjab. Our Political Parties
have never mandated the Security agencies against such ex-
tremist forces owing to their close linkages with them by a few
political parties who have never condemned these elements
rather supported them privately. After APS attack, Political
parties gave go head to Paramilitary forces to launch Operation
after adopting National Action Plan and establishing NACTA.

Pakistan Army has given unprecedented sacrifices for the
defence of the country but Americans remained stuck to do
more and same narrative of "Do More" prompted American
President Donald Trump to blame Pakistan Through tweet
that Pakistan has deceived the US despite being paid billions in
Security Aid. That blame stirred widespread protests against Us
in Pakistan by various Parties. Even, ISPR Chief Major General
Asif Ghafoor said that the aid they received is just $225 Million,
not Billion. Even, the then PML-N Government was on the
same page with ISPR and decided to review and reshape their
Policy with new and equal terms of Engagement with the US
but unfortunately that did not materialize since it was too late
for them to respond as there was no Foreign Minister in PML-N
Government for almost four years, only Sartaj Aziz worked as
Advisor to PM on Foreign Affairs . Pakistan did fail in devising
an independent foreign Policy due to being the recipient of
Security aid from the US and they stood Mum over the issue
for several days until the regular debate on Electronic Media
compelled them to clarify and respond to the allegations that
rocked the country's supremacy and Respect amongst world
Nations.

Now, when PTI has emerged as Single majority Party at Centre and likely to form Govt in Center, Punjab, KPK and Coalition Government in Baluchistan, It has great opportunity to devise an independent Foreign Policy for Pakistan to boost up its image Internationally and building Trade ties with neighbours. In his Victory Speech, Imran Khan envisaged his Foreign Policy that he intends to extend and economic connectivity in the region and beyond. In the Foreign Policy of PTI led Government, Saudi Arab and Iran will have central role followed by Old friend China. He resolved to maintain friendly relations with China and continue the CPEC projects for Infrastructural Development of Pakistan. He said that relationship with Saudi Arab and Iran will benefit Pakistan on ideological grounds and help improve Pakistan economically.

He also Envisaged US-Pak Relations on equality basis which may be beneficial for both Nations rather than the imposition over other. Especially, Imran Khan's interests in maintaining Stability in Afghanistan as except this, there would be looming security threats for Pakistan. Pakistan envisages engagement with Washington on equality basis and as a key ally to the US on basis of Mutual interest and trust.

He aspired that there should be peace in Afghanistan so that we have open borders with Afghanistan for trade as Afghanistan is a landlocked Country and it has only option to have traded through Pakistan.

About relations with India, he had the clear position that Pakistan wants Trade with India and other neighbours but the Kashmir issue has the central role. He offered India for dialogue to discuss the issue on Table Talks rather than indulging in Blame Game for Internal incidents. He stressed that the trade between Pakistan and India will mutually benefit both countries. Since PTI's main objective is to revive the Pakistan economy and decrease the growing foreign Debt and boosting and attracting investments in the country. He went on to say that If India advances one Step forward, I would advance two steps as it is very important for the people of Kashmir that the issue must be resolved through Dialogue to pave the way for the trade.

Let's hope that if PTI led Government reshapes the Foreign Policy of Pakistan and the Terms of Engagement with Neighbors and big powers i.e US, China and Russia , it will have far-reaching effects and Pakistan will reap the benefits of Regional Connectivity and revival of Economy provided that the New envisioned Policy is implemented in letter and spirit . Since it is the right time to do every possible attempt and utilize every possible option to revive the economy and bringing in foreign investments and getting rid of foreign Debt.

Imran Khan's Foreign Policy Vision has been welcomed by the world especially Saudi Arab, Iran, India, US, China and Afghanistan and all the countries showed their resolve to extend bilateral relations with New PTI Government of Pakistan. Even, Afghan President, Ashraf Ghani through his tweet confirmed that he had a Telephonic conversation with Imran Khan and have extended the invitation to Imran Khan to pay his kind Visit to Afghanistan and reiterated his stance to extend bilateral relations. The similar gesture was also shown by Saudi Arab, Iran, China, US and India through their Ambassadors and foreign Office Spokesmen.

There is also a plan in the ranks of PTI to invite all the SAARC Member Nations" PMs ,Presidents including Indian PM Narendra Modi , Afghan President ,Ashraf Ghani , Saudi

Arab Prince , Turkish President Erdogan to participate in oath taking ceremony of Imran Khan as PM of Pakistan but PTI's spokesman Mehmood-ul Rashid confirmed that such development is in pipeline and it will be discussed in the meeting after the process of formation of Governments in center, Punjab and KP .

www.ingramcontent.com/pod-product-compliance
Lightning Source LLC
Chambersburg PA
CBHW040241240726
48664CB00001B/220